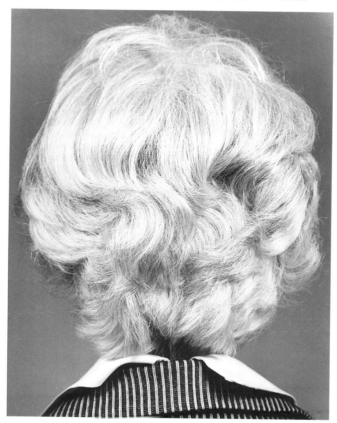

Thomas Annan

PHOTOGRAPHS OF THE OLD CLOSES AND STREETS OF GLASGOW 1868/1877

Thomas Annan

PHOTOGRAPHS OF THE OLD CLOSES AND STREETS OF GLASGOW 1868/1877

WITH A SUPPLEMENT OF 15 RELATED VIEWS

With a New Introduction by
ANITA VENTURA MOZLEY
Curator of Photography, Stanford University Museum of Art

Published through the Cooperation of
The International Museum of Photography/George Eastman House
Rochester, New York

DOVER PUBLICATIONS, INC., NEW YORK

Published in Canada by General Publishing Company, Ltd., 30 Lesmill Road, Don Mills, Toronto, Ontario.

Published in the United Kingdom by Constable and Company, Ltd., 10 Orange Street, London WC2H 7EG.

Photographs of the Old Closes and Streets of Glasgow, 1868/1877, with a Supplement of Fifteen Related Views is a new work, first published by Dover Publications, Inc., in New York, in 1977. It includes all 40 photographs by Thomas Annan from the 1878/1879 edition of *Photographs of Old Closes, Streets, & etc. taken 1868–1877*, published by the Glasgow City Improvement Trust, as well as 15 photographs from the 1900 edition, *Old Closes & Streets, a Series of Photogravures, 1868–1899*, published by James Maclehose & Sons, Publishers to the University, Glasgow. Anita Ventura Mozley has written a new Introduction especially for the Dover edition.

International Standard Book Number:
0-486-23442-8
Library of Congress Catalog Card Number:
76-27495

Manufactured in the United States of America
Dover Publications, Inc.
180 Varick Street
New York, N.Y. 10014

INTRODUCTION
TO THE DOVER EDITION

*"Be careful to avoid living in dark, damp and confined cellars;
or in backstreets adjoining to privies, or heaps of offensive and
corrupted matter; and to avoid overcrowding in small rooms."*[1]

In 1868, Thomas Annan of Glasgow took thirty-one photographs in the closes and wynds (the narrow passageways that led off the main thoroughfares of Old Glasgow to the tenements and other dwellings of the "poorer population") that were scheduled for demolition under the Glasgow City Improvements Act of 1866. Annan was then thirty-nine, and proprietor of a studio on Hope Street, in the business district of the city. He did not venture into these dens on his own initiative. The photographs were taken on commission from the Trustees of the Improvements scheme, who would, within two years, begin to tear down old buildings, to widen the narrow streets and create new ones, and to contract with private builders for new buildings in the eighty-eight acre area.

At least two sets of albumen prints of Annan's photographs of 1868 were bound, together with title and contents pages; they are now in the Mitchell Library, Glasgow.[2] In May of the depression year of 1877, when the Trust's operations had come to a standstill that would last for a decade,[3] the Trustees of the Improvements Act were asked to provide a set of the photographs of "various old and historical parts of Glasgow as existing previous to the commencement of the operations of the Trust" for exhibition in the Kelvingrove Park Museum. "Such photographs," the letter of request commented, "were of great and daily increasing interest, and could not fail to be a source of public gratification."[4] By July of that year, "several members of the Trust had requested copies of the series of Photographs taken some years ago of the more interesting

portions of the City, since, to a great extent demolished by the operations of the Improvement scheme."[5] The Trustees agreed to furnish albums to each member, and John Carrick, architect for the Trust, was instructed "to prepare the accompanying introductory and descriptive letterpress, and to have such supplementary photographs added to the Album as he might judge proper." In October, the Town Council asked for a bound set of Annan's photographs, and a set framed, "for hanging on the walls."[6] A request for a set of the photographs came from a different quarter, and with a special interest: the Librarian of the Medical Faculty of the University asked for a copy of "the Photographic Views of the old buildings dealt with by the Trust." While he acknowledges their historical value, he cites particularly the Faculty's interest: the bearing of the photographs "on the Medical and Sanitary history of the city."[7]

In December of 1878, the year of the failure of the City of Glasgow Bank, the Trustees agreed to have "Messrs. Nelson & Sons . . . bind the volumes of photographs, in Morocco," and to present copies to the Town Council, and to other officials associated with the Trust. A copy was to be sent to Melbourne in return for a gift of books and documents to the Mitchell Library.[8] Some time late in 1878 or early in 1879, then, the forty carbon prints of *Photographs of Old Closes, Streets, &c., taken 1868–1877*, which make up Plates 1–40 of this Dover edition, were published by the Glasgow City Improvements Trust in an edition of one hundred, quarto-size copies.[9] Although Mr. Carrick had arranged to have Annan take supplementary views, all of which emphasize the prevailing interest in historic buildings scheduled for demolition by the Trust (Plates 1, 16, 22, 23, 24, 37, 38 and 39), and probably suggested the inclusion of a photographic copy of the eighteenth-century print, "Trongate in the Olden Time" (Plate 19), the only descriptive letterpress in the 1878/1879 edition consists of titles to the individual photographs, which are retained in the captions of the present edition.

In 1900, two editions of *Old Closes and Streets, a Series of Photogravures, 1868–1899*, were published, both also in editions of 100. One was issued by James Maclehose & Sons, Publishers to the University; the other by T. & R. Annan & Sons, the photographic firm that Thomas Annan had founded in 1873,[10] when his brother Robert joined him in the business that he had first established in Glasgow in 1855. Both photogravure editions contain fifty plates; of the ten additional to the earlier publication, two were taken in 1868 or 1877 but not used in the 1878/1879 edition (Plates 20, 38); four plates used in the earlier edition were dropped (Plates 1, 25, 28 and 32); and twelve plates (one from a photograph taken in 1885, six from 1897, four from 1899 and one undated) were added. Annan died in 1887; it is possible, but not likely, that he took the photograph dated 1885 (with its "Funeral Office" sign) that is reproduced as Plate 50 in the gravure edition. The views of "Tontine Building, Trongate" (Plates 20, 41) and "Close, No. 115 High Street," are different from those of the same subjects that were published in 1878/1879. The photogravure editions are accompanied by an introductory text by the Glasgow historian William Young, who deals chiefly with the history of Glasgow, and only in passing with the sense of Annan's photographs and the operations of the Improvements Trust. For purposes of comparison and completeness, the Dover edition includes, as Plates 41–55, some plates from the 1900 edition (Plates 19, 20, and 38–48).

The motivation for the original commission, then, was probably well-summarized in Young's introduction: the desire to have a record of "many old and interesting landmarks." Certainly the request for the photographs of the central city as it had been before any demolition had taken place reflects the general concern that Glasgow was being turned into a completely nineteenth-century city, a city that "looks almost as new as Chicago."[11] The introduction to the second edition of *The Old Country Houses of the Old Glasgow Gentry*, for which Annan also made the photographic illustrations, expressed the concern: "Glasgow has seen great changes since this book was published eight years ago. A man who had lived here all his life till then might to-day be set down in many parts of the city without having an idea of where he was."[12] If the operations of the Trust were frightening to the people who called the hideous

part of the city home, they were also somewhat alarming to citizens who never ventured into the back streets. They "severed many a link with the past."[13] Annan's photographs were sought in the late 1870s, when the operations of the Trust were but half completed, as the only possible connecting link, and one that must be joined before another series of demolitions took place. In a sense, this clamor for the record was a part of the conservative spirit of the depressed period; it occurred during "the strange ebb" of activity that, it was feared, "may be quickly followed by a great tidal wave" of further change.[14]

Annan's photographs, particularly his general views of the old thoroughfares of Glasgow, do provide us with the historic record that the citizens sought and that Young describes. These are the ones in which we sense strongly the nineteenth-century architectural photographer's appreciation of "the rich, crumbly, picturesque."[15] But when Annan got closer to his subject, when he moved into the confining closes, he provided us with another sort of record: the earliest comprehensive series of photographs of an urban slum, and of the very slum that was considered the worst in Great Britain. It was this slum that was to be cleared out, not only by the entry of the railroads, but by the Glasgow City Improvements Act of 1866. The historian C. M. Allan has called this Act "the first massive municipal intervention to sweep away the most insanitary and dilapidated and archaic central urban areas and to re-plan them on a modern basis."[16]

Nathaniel Hawthorne had observed the lights and shades of Glasgow in 1856. Then American consul at Liverpool, he had come to Glasgow in May, taking the night train from the Lime Street Station. He put up at the Queen's Hotel on George Square, in the center of the city, "a better hotel than I have anywhere found in England—new, well-arranged, and with brisk attendance." On the morning after his arrival, Hawthorne

> rambled largely about Glasgow, and found it to be chiefly a modern-built city, with streets mostly wide and regular, and handsome houses and public edifices of a dark grey stone.

But then he

> went through the gate of the University, and penetrated into its enclosed courts, round which the College edifices are built. . . . The University stands in High Street, in a dense part of the town, and a very old and shabby part, too. I think the poorer classes of Glasgow excel even those in Liverpool in the bad eminence of filth, uncombed and unwashed children, drunkenness, disorderly deportment, evil smell, and all that makes city poverty disgusting.[17]

And Edwin Chadwick, compiler of the Poor Law Commissioners' Report on the *Sanitary Condition of* the *Labouring Population of Great Britain*, presented to Parliament in July, 1842, chose a wider geographical comparison in his absolute condemnation of Glasgow's slums: "It might admit of dispute," he wrote in the first section of the *Report*, which deals with the condition of residences, "but on the whole, it appeared . . . that both the structural arrangements and the condition of the population in Glasgow was the worst of any we had seen in any part of Great Britain."[18]

Annan's photographs, then, however clouded they might be by his taste for the picturesque, are not exactly of a subject recommended for nostalgic contemplation. They are, or rather, they might be, important complements to the statistics so avidly gathered during that period of growing recognition of the relation of slum conditions to debilitation and disease (statistics gathered by the doctors who served as Health Officers, by Poor Law Commissioners, by teachers and preachers who went into the wynds) and to current discussions of the history of urban redevelopment in Great Britain. Yet they are seldom used in this way, probably because few contemporary historians address themselves particularly to Glasgow in their discussions of problems attending the growth of cities in Victorian Great Britain. Asa Briggs, for instance, whose rich discussion of *Victorian Cities* "describes the booming cities and the people and problems they created" does not have a chapter on Glasgow, whose population increased five times from 1801 to 1861, and which by 1871 was second in population in Great Britain to London.[19]

Photographic picture books, on the other hand, surveys such as C.S. Minto's *Victorian and Edwardian Scotland from Old Photographs* (London, 1970), pay little tribute to Annan's series of photographs and offer scant information on his subject. This scanting of the importance of the subject in nineteenth-century photographs limits their significance. Nineteenth-century photographers, particularly photographers of architectural subjects, strove, for the most part, for "niceness" of viewpoint and proficiency in technique. Their intention was to reveal the subject as clearly as possible, and to do it "by the unerring witness of the sun." This truthful witness, this "faithful pencil of nature," constituted the advantage of photographs over earlier modes of topographical representation, those made by the faithless pencil of man. And, as Mr. Frank Howard said, in a paper given to the Liverpool Photographic Society in 1854, "buildings cannot possibly be transported into the painting room."

If the photographer were proficient in technique, the architectural subject was given as truly as it might be given; exaggeration born of personal interpretation, artistic limitation, or fashionably imposed style was not likely. Annan, whose publications prior to his original work for the Improvements Trust had been of architectural subjects (*The Painted Windows of the Glas-*

gow *Cathedral*, 1867; *Photographs of Glasgow*—a volume of thirteen views of the city, with descriptive letterpress by the Reverend A.G. Forbes, 1868),[20] was proficient in technique in the highest degree, and his viewpoint (we would call it composition) had always been "nice." That is probably why he was chosen to make a photographic record of the "old and interesting landmarks." It certainly is why his photographs of Glasgow's slums today command attention in the presently rising market for fine nineteenth-century photographs. But we deny half of the meaning of his work if we notice only the photographic quality of *Old Closes, Streets, &c.* and do not attend to the subject of the pictures—a subject which is today of urgent historical interest and contemporary relevance.

Annan was not a social reformer or investigator with a camera. He was no John Thomson, whose texts to *Street Life in London* (1877–1878) were vivified with quotations from nomads, cabmen, boardmen and flood victims "jotted down as they were uttered."[21] His work is more like that of A. & J. Bool and Henry Dixon, who took photographs for the Society for Photographing Relics of Old London in the 1870s and 1880s. But no text accompanies Annan's photographs as they were published in his lifetime. He did not interview the people who crowd the narrow alleys (which accommodate at most, as we observe in Plate 6, four adults standing almost shoulder to shoulder). Their presence in his photographs, while evidently not unwelcome to him, does not seem, either, to have been especially sought, and was probably occasioned by the imposing presence of this tall man and his cumbersome photographic apparatus from the world outside the closes.[22] Even sanitary workers, doctors and teachers feared to venture into these dens without protection.

To complete Annan's photographs of Old Glasgow, to document them, we must turn to the archives of the Improvement Trust, to reports of health officers and to temperance tracts.[23] This, if done thoroughly and exhaustively, promises a picture of the life and the time that might approach the one made by Jacob A. Riis, whose *How the Other Half Lives*, a report on the conditions of life in New York's lower East Side, was first published in 1890, with engravings taken from Riis's photographs. The similarity of many of Riis's views, who took up a camera only to use it as a tool in his investigations of urban slum life, to those by Annan taken several decades earlier, is striking; it encourages an initial attempt to provide some commentary on Annan's subject that is lacking in the *Old Glasgow* publications.[24]

Glasgow is an old city, whose legendary founding, according to William Young, was the burial of the holy man Fergus in the sixth century by St. Kentigern under a green grove near a fresh spring, in a cemetery consecrated by St. Ninian in time before record. Glasgow's cathedral and its castle, now destroyed, date to the thirteenth century, when Bishops of the See of Glasgow occupied the castle, and it was surrounded by residences of other men of the Church, who lived in the thoroughfares whose closes Annan photographed: Rottenrow, Drygate, High Street. Although we have heard Chadwick's and Hawthorne's comments on what the ancient areas of the city had become by the nineteenth century, the quality of the city before the workers of the Industrial Revolution occupied its center should be noted. William Young cites the comments of seventeenth- and eighteenth-century visitors. John Ray, who came to Glasgow around 1662, described it as "fair, large, and well built . . . the streets broad and pleasant." In 1669, it seemed to James Brome notable "for pleasantness of sight, sweetness of air, and delightfulness of its gardens and orchards, enriched with the most delicious fruits." Daniel Defoe, visiting Glasgow around 1725, found it "one of the cleanest, most beautiful, and best-built cities in Great Britain." In 1736, it was surrounded by "beautiful orchyards, abounding with fruits of all sorts, which by reason of the open and large streets send forth a pleasant and oderiferous smell."[25]

But the orchards and gardens of the tobacco merchants of the eighteenth century and their sweet smells had, by the third decade of the nineteenth century, been replaced by quite another scene and by a distinctly different odor. The merchants had by then moved to the West End of town, and their Georgian houses were let, at high profit, to immigrants from the Highlands, or from Ireland, or to countrymen of the Lowlands, who came to work in the textile mills, the chemical factories, the iron foundries and the engineering works of the city. The ancient thoroughfare of the High Street, the very precinct of the eminent anatomists, engineers and philosophers of the University, founded in 1450, were then given over to the housing of the "industrious poor," or to those who made their livings in the streets, in one way or another.

Although by 1861, Old Glasgow accommodated five times as many people as it had in 1775, the structure of the central city had not changed. By this time the population density in this area was from 500 to 1,000 people per acre. Irish immigration at the height of the potato famine had dramatically increased overcrowding in the center of the city. In the four months from December, 1848, to March, 1849, 43,000 Irish came to Glasgow to live.[26] The city suffered its third cholera epidemic in 1853–1854; 100 people per thousand died in the epidemic, a figure that Chadwick found suitable for a city devoted to "Siva the Destroyer." Old Glasgow, by 1865, the year in which the Improvements Act was proposed, recommended itself, by all contemporary accounts, to anyone's "Gazetteer of Disgusting Places."[27] In every disgusting regard—over-

building, with its attendant curtailment of ventilation and light, and overcrowding in the overbuilt buildings, with its attendant destruction of physical and moral life—Glasgow was preeminent. Because of its particular system of land sale and its lack of authority over the advantages to absentee landlords of "making down" or subdividing existing buildings, Glasgow appears to have distilled, concentrated and emphasized the ills of the Industrial Revolution as they were magnified in an urban setting.[28]

The Minute Book of Trustees under the Glasgow Improvements Act, 1866, in the "Anno Vicesimo nono Victoriae Reginae, Cap. LXXXV," gives the Preamble to "An Act for the Improvement of the City of Glasgow and the Construction of new, and widening, altering, and diverting of existing Streets in the said City; and for other Purposes":

> Whereas various Portions of the City of *Glasgow* are so built, and the Buildings thereon are so densely inhabited, as to be highly injurious to the moral and physical Welfare of the Inhabitants, and many of the thoroughfares are narrow, circuitous, and inconvenient, and it would be of public and local Advantage if various Houses and Buildings were taken down, and those portions of the said City reconstituted, and new Streets were constructed in and through various Parts of said City, and several of the existing Streets altered and widened and diverted, and that in connexion with the Reconstruction of these portions of the City Provision was made for Dwellings for the Labouring Classes who may be misplaced in consequence thereof . . .[29]

Under the act, thirty-nine new streets were to be built, twelve old ones altered, and the cleared ground was to be sold or leased to private owners who would build dwellings according to plans approved by the Trust.[30]

The Improvements Act was the culmination of attempts to change the structure and the population density, to better the living conditions from a "moral and physical" point of view. The attempts had begun under local authority in 1843, when the Dean of Guild, in the Glasgow Police Act of that year, was given power to order demolition of decayed buildings in the city.[31] In 1846, the Town Council had set aside 30,000 pounds for acquiring some of the worst and most overbuilt areas in the wynds and closes leading off from High Street and Saltmarket and in the Gorbals area, south of the Clyde.[32] In October of 1859, the Glasgow Waterworks, by which 50 million gallons of water would be daily conveyed through thirty-four miles of pipe from Loch Katrine to the city, was opened by Queen Victoria, who noted "the spirit of enterprize and philanthropy of Glasgow" in her remarks, and declared that the waterworks "are calculated to improve the health and comfort of that vast population which is rapidly increasing round the great centre of manufacturing industry in Scotland."[33] The Glasgow Police Act of 1862 was the first municipal act to grapple with the evil of overcrowding of the rapidly increasing population. It gave the police the power to measure cubic contents of "any house [i.e., flat] consisting of 'not more than three apartments' [i.e., rooms], and if the cubic contents were 2,000 to affix a ticket on which the cubic space and the number of inmates proportioned thereto is stated. All such houses may thereafter be visited at night, and a fine imposed for an excess of inmates."[34] Even so, the cubic space allowed for each adult and for two children under eight was small: 300 cubic feet, which comes to, in terms of square footage in an 8-foot-high room, a floor area only 6 feet square.

The railroads, too, played their part in the achievement of the act. After almost twenty years of considering the move, the University finally quitted its old precincts in the High Street. The move was determined partly by the desire for more commodious and pleasant surroundings, and partly by the insistent approach of the railroads into central Glasgow. The role of the railroads as an instrument of housing reform was dramatically stated in testimony on the advisability of a route through Old Glasgow: the route would be "the kind of improvement so much needed. It will pull down the poor class of house and ventilate that part of the City which is very much overcrowded."[35] By 1865, Glasgow had the financial power, as well as the will (born of the fear of epidemic disease, a philanthropic sense and civic pride), to apply to Parliament for the enactment of a redevelopment scheme.

While an antiquarian interest occasioned the making of Annan's photographs of the areas to be demolished by the Trustees of the Improvements Act, the Act itself was "the first recognition that a free market and private philanthropy and public health regulation could not provide an adequate solution to overcrowded slums."[36] Annan's photographs of these slums become of more than antiquarian interest when materials in the Archives of the Corporation of Glasgow are referred to. Readings of the *Minute Book of Trustees*, the Trust architect's *Books of Reference to the Plans of the Lands, Houses and Other Property proposed to be purchased ... for the purpose of the said Improvements and New Streets*, and Glasgow City Directories of the period, make possible some initial documentation of Annan's views and also illuminate the working of the Trust. The *Book of Reference* for Areas A. to R. in the scheme was drawn up in November, 1865; it consists of a map of central Glasgow, with areas discussed shown in blue, the modifications and changes proposed indicated in red; and it contains the names of the owners, lessees and occupiers of the lands in which changes are proposed. Documents that pertain, for example, to Annan's

Plate 16, "Old Building, High Street," describe it as being in area P. of the architect's plan book, an area in the "City Parish of Glasgow and *Quoad Sacra* Parish of St. Paul or Outer High." The building to the left in the photograph is noted by John Carrick, the architect, as "4 storey old." It was let to Bernard Hair, a pawn-broker, and William Ferguson, "drysalter, oil and colourman," according to the City Directory. The building, No. 58 on the architect's plan, is described as "shops, dwelling houses, pawn office, cellars, court, passage, privy and ashbin." Five people were reputed to have owned it, and twelve men's names are given as occupiers. In addition to the twelve are the women and children of Annan's photographs, who also occupied and used the "cellars, court, privy," and so forth. Their names will not figure in City Directories, nor will those of their lodgers; it is possible that some might be known from sanitation reports. What is suggested here is a beginning of an attempt to flesh out Annan's pictures, to give the people in them an identity and a voice.

As the lands that came under the Improvement scheme's authority were purchased, Mr. Carrick submitted to the Trustees his committee's proposals for them. Typical entries in the *Minute Book*, typical in both their hopes and in the realization of the limitations of their efforts, follow:

> The purchase of Ground for houses for the labouring classes has been completed, and plans have been prepared, showing houses of one apartment, room and kitchen, and two rooms and kitchen. These plans have been repeatedly gone over, and your Committee have made various suggestions as to them. As the plans now stand, they provide much better and far more airy accommodation of the different classes above mentioned than could be obtained at present, and, as they believe, the rents will be less than what is now paid for inferior accommodations ... as soon as the tenants can be dealt with.[37]

And this as well:

> Statistics have been carefully prepared, showing the number of the working class who will be displaced by these operations, and also the number of houses of one, two and three apartments at present in the course of erection, and your Committee are satisfied that ample accommodation will be ready by Whitsunday for all who will be displaced....[38]

The main point of the Improvements scheme, the bettering of conditions in regard to ventilation, light and density of occupation in the buildings, is constantly sounded in Mr. Carrick's proposals to the Trustees and in their responses to his proposals:

> Mr. Carrick submitted plans of the two Blocks now proposed to be dealt with, showing the proposed alterations, and stated that the number of persons requiring to be displaced in the two Areas [the east side of Saltmarket between St. Andrew Street and

Steel Street, and between Bell Street and Stirling Street] would be under or about 300—And the Committee having considered the same, approve thereof, and authorize the operations to be proceeded with accordingly, they being merely the taking down of various back properties to allow light and air into the remainder, and render them fit for habitation in a sanitary point of view, until the blocks are re-modeled.[39]

By 1874, Dr. James Burn Russell, Medical Officer of Health, reported in a paper read before the Sanitary Section of the Philosophical Society that "since 1870, the Improvement Trust has, from time to time, demolished the houses of some 15,425 persons," and that since 1866, "no less than 26,794 houses had been built." From data taken on 900 inhabitants of 243 houses (flats of one and two rooms), Dr. Russell found that, generally, "the result of the intervention of the Improvement Trust" had been beneficial to the families in his study.[40]

Yet, Russell warned, the conditions that led to the enactment of the scheme still pertained, and would continue, so long as the Dean of Guild Court lacked sufficient power to prevent overbuilding. Lacking this power, the landlords of the mid-1870s could not be prevented, as their predecessors in the area had not been, from acceding to the demands of the poor for small and inexpensive housing. They would continue to make-down their houses and to thus create new tenements. While he found that "the operations of the Improvement Trust must in themselves be productive of good, inasmuch as they expel, from circumstances than which none worse could be found or imagined, a body of morally debased and physically deteriorated inhabitants, and make straight and spacious thoroughfares, in place of cramped and inconvenient wynds and closes . . . ," he believed that "the operations of the Improvement Trust against the 'moral and physical' evils alluded to in the preamble to the Act, depend for their thorough success on support from other parts of the field. . . . we must see to it, that we are not building up with the one hand houses which may, for want of sufficient restrictive and regulative power, become as bad in process of time as those which we are pulling down with the other."

The conditions necessary to ensure the success of the act, and to prevent the return of "the evils it is intended to remove" were still measures that would make impossible overcrowding in all its forms: of "tenements on the soil, or over-building," of "dwelling houses in the tenement and internal defects of structure," and of too many "inhabitants in the dwelling house." Still, in the mid 1870s, eight years after the enactment of a Public Health (Scotland) Act, Russell could declare that these evils "are cognate, found together, intensify the evil effects of the other, and produce that state of

chronic ill-health, with acute exacerbations, which is a feature of the life of Glasgow."[41]

By this time, the Trustees of the Improvements Act, using their powers to borrow and to tax, had bought 77 acres, occasionally with compulsory power. Within two years, by 1877, when the demand for land disappeared, the Trust had no income, since the cleared land had no takers. The Trust could not, therefore, proceed with clearing the remaining land under its schedule. By the time Annan took the second series of photographs of *Old Closes, Streets, &c.*, those of 1877, the Trust had become, in effect, a slum landlord.

The ebb tide of the Trust's operations finally turned in 1889, when, in the first phase of what has been called "municipal socialism," the Trust itself embarked upon municipal rebuilding, a "program of demolition and building [so vigorous] . . . that by 1902, the work of the 1866 Act was completed." By that time it had built 1,646 houses and 394 shops and building premises. The workings of the Trust benefited chiefly those working poor who afforded the higher price asked for flats with light, water and inside closets. But the buildings it put up did not solve the problem of Glasgow's slums, which moved to farther boundaries, and the substantial buildings it erected became slums themselves, through obsolescence, rather than decay. While the historical importance of the scheme lies in its comprehensiveness, that comprehensiveness almost completely demolished the physical evidence of Glasgow's "great pre-nineteenth century trading, commercial and academic heritage."[42]

It is no coincidence, then, that the second publication of *Old Closes and Streets of Glasgow*, the photogravure edition of 1900, was published near the end of the second phase of change in the city's heart, just as the 1878/1879 edition had been brought out at the close of the first period of the Improvement Trust's activity.

Annan's photographs of Glasgow's *Old Closes, Streets, &c.*, were published in carbon, one of the several "permanent" processes available in the 1870s. The impermanence of photographic prints had been a bugaboo to practitioners of the art from the beginnings of photography. As the *Illustrated London News* put it,

Beautiful, interesting, and in some respects invaluable as are the productions in photography, there is one fatal drawback to their value—namely, that their continuance cannot be depended upon; on the contrary, that in all probability they must all, sooner or later, fade away. What the sun gives, the sun will take away, and there seems to have been no certain means devised under the ordinary process to avert this cruel destiny.[43]

The remarks were made upon the publication of a carbon process by Mr. John Pouncy, of Dorchester, for whom a subscription was taken, headed by the Prince

Consort, to repay him for his trouble in developing a process that promised to avert the cruel action of the sun on silver prints. There had been other milestones, both French and British, in the development of the carbon printing of photographic negatives, a process that depended upon an observation made by the Scotsman, Mungo Ponton, in 1839, that bichromate of potassium spread on paper is light-sensitive.

But carbon printing did not attract wide attention in the photographic world until Joseph Swan, of Newcastle-on-Tyne, exhibited "specimens of prints by a new carbon process, from which it appeared that Mr. Swan had solved the problem of permanent printing, as they were equal in every respect to the finest prints produced by nitrate of silver."[44] The process, as Swan presented it to the Photographic Society of London on April 15, 1864, was not analogous to any printing-press process, but to silver printing. The chemical principal that it depended upon was Ponton's discovery, "that gelatine, in combination with a salt of chromium, becomes insoluble in water after a short exposure to sunlight."[45] A brief description of the process is given in the Society's *Journal* for September 15, 1864:

> A solution of gelatine is coloured by the additions of indian ink or lampblack, and some other pigments, such as crimson lake and indigo, to modify the tone. This is applied to sheets of paper, and dried. When required for use, the paper is floated, gelatine side down, on a solution of bichromate of potash for a few moments, much in the same way in which albuminized paper is rendered sensitive in the nitrate-of-silver bath. When dry, the paper is printed under a negative, the prepared side being in contact. The object is now to wash away all the gelatine, colour, &c., which have not been acted upon by light; but these are at the opposite side of the film, and in contact with the paper. The print is then mounted, gelatine side down, on to fresh paper, with some material that will be insoluble in water. This done, the whole is plunged in warm water; and the gelatine which is not rendered insoluble being quickly softened, the original paper on which it had rested is released and floats off, whilst the coating remains attached by the insoluble cement to the paper on which it was last mounted, and is there developed.

In its early use, this method produced prints of high contrast. They lacked the fine gradation of halftones that was one of the glories of photographic prints. But Swan overcame this problem, as well as that of large-scale application of the process. In 1866, after refining his method and coping with the questioning of his right to patent the process, he set up a printing establishment at Newcastle-on-Tyne, where he produced editions from a single negative of at least 1,000 carbon prints, in large sizes that had previously been impossible.

Swan's first major publication, and Annan's working introduction to carbon printing, was in June, 1866, when Swan printed the negatives Annan had made the previous year of David Octavius Hill's huge canvas, "The Signing of the Deed of Demission," for which Hill, with Robert Adamson, had made calotype portraits in 1843 in Edinburgh. Annan used a camera that had been designed especially for the task; Dallmeyer, the famous lensmaker of London, designed the lens. The photographs were taken out of doors; Swan printed them in three sizes, the largest being 48 x 21¼ inches, each in editions of 1,000.[46] In the same year, Annan purchased from Swan the rights to practice his carbon process in Scotland.

In 1878, when Swan's patent for the manufacture of the pigmented tissue used in the process had lapsed, Annan set up an extensive printing establishment at Lenzie, where the edition of *Old Closes, Streets, &c.* was printed. It was there, too, that he printed the second edition of *Old Country Houses,* and large prints for exhibition, such as his well-known *Dumbarton Castle.* His enlarging facilities enabled him to print enormous negatives: John Nicol reported, in 1878, that he "saw what most photographers would admit was a large negative, being a copy of a picture on a plate seven feet by three and a-half feet."[47] It is clear from Nicol's report that Annan had established at Lenzie, as Swan had at Newcastle, and George Washington Wilson at Aberdeen, a commercial printing establishment that can be compared to those of today that produce photographic murals for exhibition.

Annan's carbon prints, as seen in *Old Closes, Streets, &c.* are of a rich black-brown color; the matt surface is quite unlike that of albumen prints of the same period, with their slight gloss and precise detail. The carbon prints resemble, rather, a well-fixed chalk or charcoal drawing. They are broad, rather than precise, in detail; massive is a word that comes to mind, and they seem appropriate to the massive stone that built the houses and lined the pavements of Glasgow's slums. The comparison is not without irony: while permanence in photographic prints is desirable, the permanence of the building material of Glasgow's tenements is even now problematical.

Annan's approach was not what we would call straight. This is disappointing to us today, when we recognize a style called documentary. He added clouds, which brighten the skies over Glasgow's slums, and he whitened the wash on the line. He did this for pictorial effect, for nice balance. While his taste for the picturesque, for a tradition inherited from painting, and quite in accord with salon practice of the day, may distort to some extent the immediacy of the *mise-en-scène,* we must appreciate the fact that he did not tidy up the rest of the picture, as his son, James Craig Annan, did when he made the photogravure plates for the 1900 edition. The photogravures are lighter in tone, and consequently in mood, in the sense of the place, than

Annan's carbon prints. Moving figures, those ghosts who would not stand still for the photographer, are completely excised in the photogravure edition; and the black hole that is so eloquent a metaphor of Thomas Annan's series of pictures, in his Plate 29, "Close, No. 61 Saltmarket" of 1868, is drawn into, and printed with detail in the 1900 edition.

It is likely that Annan regarded the commission from the Trustees of the Improvements Act as just another he received when his success as a commercial photographer of Glasgow was increasingly recognized. However inadvertently, he did give us the first thorough photographic representation available of the dwelling places and the inhabitants of an urban slum. But the appreciation of this work of his has grown only recently; at his death, he was chiefly remembered for his work as a copier of paintings, and for his personal qualities. In the photographic world, these were closely intertwined with his introduction of permanent processes of printing, an appreciation that we, so used to halftone reproduction, may find difficult to understand. While his obituary in the *British Journal of Photography* of December 23, 1887, omitted mention of his *Old Closes, Streets, &c.*, and of his contemporary pre-eminence in landscape views, it mentioned especially his excellence in the reproduction of paintings, his faithful translation of "some masterpiece into monochrome through the medium of his camera." There is certainly a paradox implicit in this excerpt from the *Journal's* obituary of the man who took the first comprehensive views of a nineteenth-century urban slum and its inhabitants:

> Honourable in feeling, and fastidious in taste, he was utterly intolerant of shams, and of everything below the best. It was natural that he should have felt dissatisfied with the uncertain permanence of silver prints, and been one of the first to introduce carbon printing, and that, later, he should have gone a step further in the direction of permanent printing by taking up photogravure.

But if the *Journal's* obituary emphasizes Annan's superb technical ability, and if I have discussed at length the importance of his subject, we should remember that these are interesting because the photographs are themselves so worthy of attention. It is their power and beauty, after all, that moves us to know all that we can of their technique and their subject.

NOTES

1. An address by the Manchester Board of Health to the poor, 1799. Quoted in E.P. Hennock, "Urban Sanitary Reform a Generation before Chadwick?", *Economic History Review*, Vol. X, No. 1, 1957, p. 113. And the Board suggested to the landlords that their tenants would be less subject to disease and therefore more able to pay their rents if the problems cited above were remedied.

2. Jerald C. Maddox, Curator of Photography of the Library of Congress, kindly supplied me with notes on these albums in the Mitchell Library as well as with notes from the *Minute Book of Trustees under the Glasgow Improvement Act, 1866,* in the Glasgow Corporation Archives, and with important references to Annan and his work in the *British Journal of Photography.* Without Mr. Maddox's research, the history of the publication of *Old Closes, Streets &c.* could not be given here; and the paper on which this introduction is based, given at a Symposium on the Art History of Photography, held at the International Museum of Photography, George Eastman House, Rochester, N.Y., in February, 1975, would have been impossible. Notes supplied by Mr. Maddox are prefixed by "J.M." and include the sources, as he has given them to me, of his information.

3. C.M. Allan, "The Genesis of British Urban Redevelopment with special reference to Glasgow," *Economic History Review*, Second Series, Vol. XVII, No. 3, 1965, p. 606.

4. J.M.: *Minute Book,* May 16, 1877.

5. J.M.: *ibid.,* July 25, 1877.

6. J.M.: *ibid.,* October 3, 1877.

7. J.M.: *ibid.,* October 17, 1877.

8. J.M.: *ibid.,* December 11, 1878.

9. J.M.: *British Journal of Photography,* April 19, 1878. In an article entitled "Notes from the North," John Nicol, who figures in the Trustees' requests to have prints of Annan's photographs made, had "the pleasure in publishing a few notes of a late visit to the carbon printing establishment of Mr. Annan, of Glasgow, recently erected at Lenzie . . . a village some six or eight miles to the east of Glasgow," a place "better suited for such work than the smoky city." Annan showed Mr. Nicol some of the "few little jobs" he modestly admitted to having in hand. Among them were "3,000 prints from thirty negatives of the old closes and other interesting portions of Glasgow now removed by the Improvement Trust to make way for more modern erections." No mention is made, in the interview, of the ten other negatives published in carbon prints in *Photographs of Old Closes, Streets, &c.*

10. M.F. Harker, "Annans of Glasgow," *British Journal of Photography*, October 19, 1873, p. 966.

11. Introduction to the 1870 edition, *The Old Country Houses of the Old Glasgow Gentry,* illustrated by permanent photographs by Annan, Glasgow, James Maclehose, 1878, p. xi. Another introduction, written for the second edition, is also given.

12. *Ibid.,* p. xiv. I am grateful to Ann Turner, producer of the BBC-TV series, "Pioneer Photographers," for bringing this publication of Annan's photographs to my attention, and for supplying me with the texts from which these quotations are taken.

13. *Ibid.*

14. *Ibid.,* p. xvi,

15. A phrase used in commending the architectural photography of Francis Bedford in a review of an exhibition of his photographs in 1862.

16. Allan, *op. cit.,* p. 613.

17. Nathaniel Hawthorne, *Our Old Home, and English Note-Books,* Vol. II, from Vol. VIII, *The Complete Works of Nathaniel Hawthorne,* Riverside Edition, Boston and New York, 1887, pp. 246–247. Yet Hawthorne could say, on the morning after his "ramble," when he "walked out and saw something of the newer portion" of Glasgow, that, after all, "I am inclined to think it the stateliest of cities." The problem was confined to the old center of the city. In Hawthorne's mind, evidently, the "bad eminence of filth" was quite blotted out by the better conditions in the residential West End.

Thomas Annan

PHOTOGRAPHS OF THE OLD CLOSES AND STREETS OF GLASGOW 1868/1877

PLATE 1. Head of High Street

PLATE 2. Old Vennel, off High Street

PLATE 3. Broad Close, No. 167 High Street

PLATE 4. High Street, from College Open

PLATE 5. Close, No. 148 High Street

PLATE 6. Close, No. 118 High Street

PLATE 7. Close, No. 115 High Street

PLATE 8. Close, No. 101 High Street

PLATE 9. Close, No. 193 High Street

PLATE 10. Close, No. 83 High Street

PLATE 11. Close, No. 80 High Street

PLATE 12. Close, No. 75 High Street

PLATE 13. Close, No. 65 High Street

PLATE 14. Bell Street, from High Street

PLATE 15. Close, No. 37 High Street

PLATE 16. Old Building, High Street

PLATE 17. High Street, from the Cross

PLATE 18. Trongate, from Tron Steeple

PLATE 19. Trongate in the Olden Time

PLATE 20. Tontine Building, Trongate

PLATE 21. Close, No. 29 Gallowgate

PLATE 22. King Street

PLATE 23. Laigh Kirk Close

PLATE 24. Princes Street, from King Street

PLATE 25. Close, No. 18 Saltmarket

PLATE 26. Close, No. 28 Saltmarket

PLATE 27. Close, No. 30 Saltmarket

PLATE 28. Close, No. 46 Saltmarket

PLATE 29. Close, No. 61 Saltmarket

PLATE 30. Closes, Nos. 97 and 103 Saltmarket

PLATE 31. Close, No. 122 Saltmarket

PLATE 32. Close, No. 128 Saltmarket

PLATE 33. Close, No. 136 Saltmarket

PLATE 34. Close, No. 139 Saltmarket

PLATE 35. Saltmarket, from Bridgegate

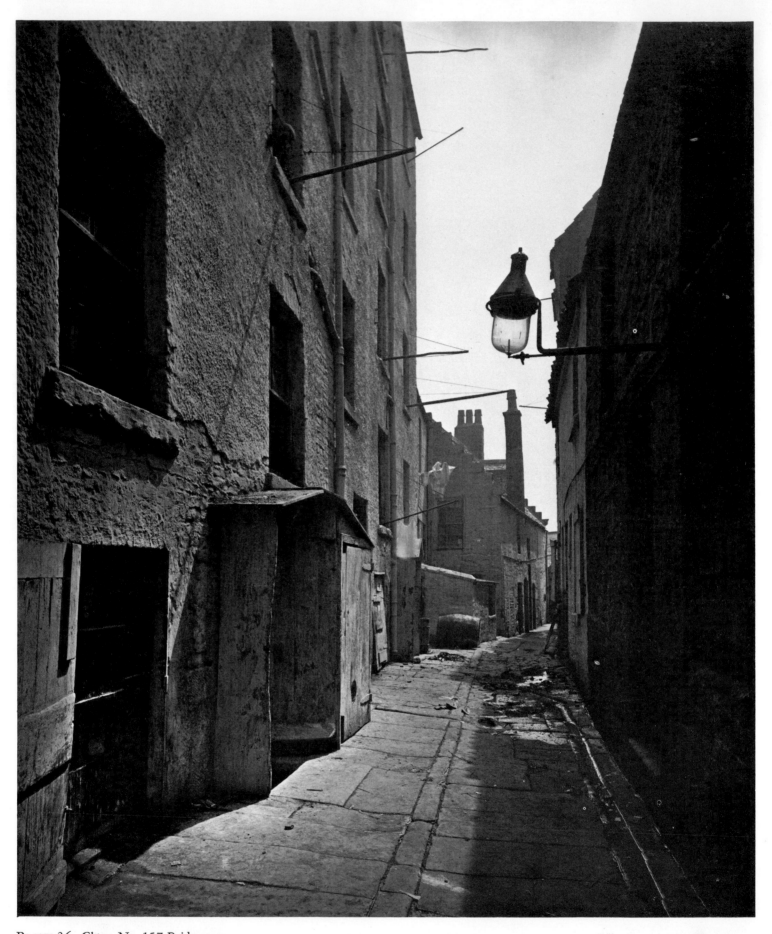

PLATE 36. Close, No. 157 Bridgegate

PLATE 37. Low Green Street

PLATE 38. Clothes Market, foot of Saltmarket

PLATE 39. Main Street, Gorbals, looking South

PLATE 40.   Main Street, Gorbals, looking North

PLATE 41. Tontine Building, Trongate, 1868 (Plate 19, 1900 edition)

PLATE 42. Gallowgate, 1868 (Plate 20, 1900 Edition)

PLATE 43. Elphinstone Tower, Main Street, Gorbals, 1868 (Plate 38, 1900 Edition)

PLATE 44. Corner of Duke Street and High Street, 1897 (Plate 39, 1900 Edition)

PLATE 45. Old Houses at Corner of George Street and High Street (Plate 40, 1900 Edition)

PLATE 46. Close, No. 267 High Street, 1897 (Plate 41, 1900 Edition)

PLATE 47. Close, No. 29 Bridgegate, 1897 (Plate 42, 1900 Edition)

PLATE 50. St. Margaret's Place, 1897 (Plate 45, 1900 Edition)

PLATE 51. Nelson Street, City, 1899 (Plate 46, 1900 Edition)

PLATE 52. Back Wynd from Trongate, 1899 (Plate 47, 1900 Edition)

PLATE 53. The Back Wynd, 1899 (Plate 48, 1900 Edition)

PLATE 54. Bridgegate from Corner of Market Street, 1899 (Plate 49, 1900 Edition)

PLATE 55. Saltmarket from London Street, 1885 (Plate 50, 1900 Edition)